No. #1 Energy Audit Reference Book

By Vinay Saketh Nidamarthi ∞

For Energy Audit Professionals: Contains useful tables and formulae for ready reference.

PREFACE

Welcome to this comprehensive reference guide on energy audits specifically tailored for electrical systems. This book is designed to serve as an essential onsite resource for electrical engineers, energy managers, energy auditors and professionals involved in energy optimization. Whether you're conducting your first energy audit or seeking to refine your approach with the latest methodologies, this guide aims to provide you with the necessary tools and insights.

Energy audits are pivotal in identifying inefficiencies and understanding energy consumption patterns within electrical installations. This book integrates insights from established leaders in electrical engineering, ensuring you have access to a wide array of expert knowledge and real-world applications.

This is the first edition of the book, and it will evolve with contributions from its readers. We encourage you to share your experiences and suggestions to enhance future editions. Please feel free to contact us at auditreferencebook@gmail.com with your feedback and updates.

Furthermore, this book is a tribute to personal inspiration and support. It is **dedicated to my mother and father**, whose unwavering support made this endeavor possible. Their encouragement has been a guiding light in the pursuit of this project.

We hope this book will be a valuable addition to your professional toolkit, helping you achieve significant energy and cost savings while advancing towards our collective goal of environmental sustainability. Thank you for choosing this guide, and we look forward to your contributions to its continuous improvement.

Nidamarthi Vinay Saketh
B.Tech (EEE)

Contents

Important Points: 4

Important Relation: 5

Specific Energy Consumption of Designated Consumers 6

    Benchmarking for Thermal Power Plants [3] 6

    Benchmarking for Cement Industry [3] 6

    Benchmarking for Fertilizer Industry [3] 6

    Benchmarking for Aluminium Industry [3] 6

    Benchmarking for Iron and Steel Industry [3] 7

    Benchmarking for Chlor-alkali Industry [3] 7

    Benchmarking for Pulp and Paper [3] 7

    Benchmarking for Indian Building [3] 8

Transformers 9

    MV/LV ABB Transformer Losses [4] 9

    Oil type distribution transformer 10

    Oil type generator transformer at power plant, LV Voltage depends on generation voltage 10

    MV/LV Transformer Losses for Dry type transformer [5] 11

    MV/LV ABB Transformer typical inrush currents (kA) for oil transformers [4] 11

    MV/LV ABB Transformer typical inrush currents (kA) for Cast resin transformer [4] 12

Motors 13

    Typical Efficiency of LV Induction Motor [6] 13

    IE 3 LV Motor Parameters as per IEC 60034-30-1 : 2014 [7] 14

    IE 4 LV Motor Parameters as per IEC 60034-30-1: 2014 [7] 15

    LV DC Motor Parameters as per IEC 60034-1 [8] 16

    LV Adjustable Speed Drive Part load Efficiency (VFD Efficiency) 17

    Motor Performance with an unbalanced Utilization Voltage [9] 17

    Effect of Applied Voltage Variation on Motor Performance - IEEE 141-1993 Standard [10] 17

    % Harmonic – Voltage in MV and LV Distribution IEC 61000 [1] 18

    Typical Losses in an Induction Motor [11] 18

    Typical Stray Losses in a Induction Motor [12] 18

    Allowable Number of Motor Starts and Minimum Time between starts. [9] 19

    Analysis of Motor Failures [13] 19

Capacitor 22

    Switching technologies for MV capacitor banks [14] 22

    ABB Motors , kVAr Compensation at Motor terminals [4] 22

    ABB Transformer required compensation in kVAr [4] 23

    Power Factor Correction Chart 24

Industrial Cables 25

    Current Ratings of XLPE Insulated Conductor [15] 25

    Current rating (D.C.) for Two single core cable with XLPE Insulation and rated voltage 1500 V [15] 26

    Derating factor for variation in ambient air for cables [15] 26

    Current Ratings of XLPE Insulated Conductor [15] 27

    Derating Factor for two single core cable laid in ground, horizontal formation (DC) [15] 27

    Derating Factor for multi core cable laid in ground, horizontal formation [15] 28

    Derating Factor for three core cable laid in duct, horizontal formation [15] 28

    Conversion table for AWG to Sq.mm 29

    Grounding Conductor Sizing char at Terminal of Motors [2] 30

    Typical power factors of some electrical equipment [4] 31

UPS 31

    UPS Efficiency at different loads. 31

    Energy Efficiency in Conveyors 32

    Energy Efficiency in Hydraulics [16] 32

    Energy Efficiency in Cranes 33

    Energy Efficiency in HVAC 33

Advances in Sustainable Convertor/Inverter Technology 33

    Three phase Static Stabilizers 33

    Direct Torque Control Drives 33

Advances in Sustainable Motor Technology 34

    Electrostatic Motors 34

    Synchronous Reluctance Motors (SyRM) 34

Advances in Sustainable Battery Technology 35

    Aloe vera Batteries: 35

    AC Battery 35

Emission Factors for Greenhouse Gas Inventories- Stationary Combustion [17] 36

Emission Factors for Greenhouse Gas Inventories- Mobile Combustion [17] 38

Types of Hydrogen 39

Hydrogen Fueled Powered Power Plants [12] 39

City in India and relative climate zones [5] 40

USEFUL SOFTWARE'S AND CALCULATORS 41

References 44

- In Transformers the thumb rule is "The lower the operating frequency the more flux lines that are generated in core", so a transformer rated at 60Hz should not be operated on a 50Hz due to higher losses and core saturation(it can be operated if %loading is less and also forced cooling with continuous monitoring is present), But a transformer rated at 50 Hz can run cooler in 60Hz operating frequency.

- kVAr required to achieve unity PF $= kW_{Load} \times \left(\sqrt{1 - \frac{1}{PF^2}} \right)$

- Improving power factor at user-end reduces the distribution losses due to poor PF.

- In Overspeed condition, the torque decreases because impedance increases with frequency and please check bearing's design speed before over speeding operation.

- If you need to cross check a reading and no VFD is present then power can be calculated from **Ammeter** i.e., assuming temperature of medium is $< 35\,^\circ$C and for a LV Motor (Considering η=87%), ensure no PF compensation is provided at motor.

  - 70%-90% Loading, kW = 0.56 x Measured Amps

  - 25%-40% Loading, kW = 0.26 x Measured Amps

- If you need to cross check a reading (no VFD on motor) based on % Loading (**Onsite Reading**) for a LV Motor (~ η=87%), This applicable for hydraulic pumps, compressors, conveyors. Etc:

  - If motor 25%-40% loaded, then estimated kW = 0.31 x Rated kW.

  - If motor 70%-87% loaded, then estimated kW = 0.71 X Rated kW.

- Dual speed motors use a combination of a Dahlander winding with a single winding or more.

- All slipring motors can be operated on VFD by shorting the sliprings.

- The Arc of DC Arc Furnace's is more stable than arc in AC Arc furnaces [1]

Important Relation:

1. Transformer All-day Efficiency $= \dfrac{kW.Hrs.Output\ in\ 24\ Hrs}{kW.Hrs.Output + kW.Hrs.Wasted\ in\ 24\ Hrs}$

2. Rating of Booster Transformer $= Load\ KVA\ \times\ \%\ Boost\ in\ Voltage$

3. Energy Performance Index (EPI) (kWh/m2. y) $= \dfrac{Annual\ Grid\ kWh + Annual\ DG\ kWh}{Built-up\ area}$

4. Average Annual hourly Energy Performance Index AAhEPI (Wh/h.m2)

$$= \dfrac{EPI\ (kWh/m2.y)\times 1000}{Annual\ hours\ of\ operation}$$

5. $I_{RMS} = I_1\sqrt{1 + THD^2}$

6. EE Motor Replacement Saving kW$_{saved}$ $= HP \times \%Loading\ \times 0.786\left(\dfrac{100}{\eta_{NE}} - \dfrac{100}{\eta_{HE}}\right)$

7. Required kVAR for an induction machine [2] $\leq \dfrac{0.9\times No\ load\ Amp\ \times Rated\ V\ \times\sqrt{3}}{1000\times(1+per\ unit\ maximum\ overspeed)^2}$

8. 3rd Harmonics flow through Neutral and elevate Neutral to ground Voltage.

9. % Voltage unbalance $= 100\ \times\ \dfrac{Maximum\ voltage\ deviation\ from\ average\ voltage}{Average\ Voltage}$

10. Torque and Power $W = \dfrac{2\pi\ \times N\ \times T}{60}$, where T $=$ torque in N-m and N $=$ RPM

11. Loss in Motor $= Input\ kW\ \times (\ 1 - \eta\ )$

12. Bearing Loss in HP [2] $= 2.4\ \times\ 10^{-8}\ \times added\ load\ in\ lbs.\times RPM\ \times$

   $pitch\ dia\ of\ balls\ in\ inches$

13. % Loading (Slip Method) $= \dfrac{Synchronous\ Speed - Measured\ Speed}{Synchronous\ Speed - NamePlate\ Speed}$

14. RPM $= \left(\dfrac{120\times f}{P}\right)$

15. The size of the fan can be determined by the following equation relating air flow in cubic feet per minute (CFM) to the power in watts (W) dissipated within the enclosure and the allowable temperature rise (DF) above ambient that can be tolerated within the enclosure.

   CFM = (3.16 X W) / DF

Specific Energy Consumption of Designated Consumers

Benchmarking for Thermal Power Plants [3]

Category	SEC (kCal/kWh)					
	Gross Unit Heat Rate (National Best)	Gross Unit Heat Rate (Average)	APC (National Best)	APC (Average)	Net Heat Rate (National Best)	Net Heat Rate (Average)
<100 MW	2606	3082	8.38%	11.18%	2908	3470
100-150 MW	2450	2718	6.92%	11.48%	2687	3070
150-300 MW	2274	2554	5.86%	7.36%	2469	2757
300-600 MW	2244	2386	6.66%	6.66%	2419	2556
Gas	1837	2161	1.43%	3.47%	1881	2239

Benchmarking for Cement Industry [3]

Particulars	Units	Global Avg.	India Best	India Average
Specific Electrical Energy Consumption	kWh/tonne of cement	91	64	80
Specific Thermal Energy Consumption	GJ/tonne of clinker	3.5	2.83	3.1

Benchmarking for Fertilizer Industry [3]

Product	SEC(Gcal/MT)		
	India (average)	India (Best)	World best
Urea	5.93	5.164	5
Ammonia	8.33	7.098	6.88

Benchmarking for Aluminium Industry [3]

Production	Global Best	Global Average	India Average	India Best Numbers	Unit
Alumina Refinery	0.2	0.267	0.33	0.23	TOE/Tonne of Alumina
Aluminium Smelting	13599	14145	14361	14558	kWh/Tonne of Molten Aluminium

Benchmarking for Iron and Steel Industry [3]

Particulars	Units	Global Best	India Best	India Average
Specific energy consumption	GCal/tcs	5.38	5.67	7.17

Benchmarking for Chlor-alkali Industry [3]

Parameters	Units	Value
Total water requirement	m³/MT NaOH	5.9
Process water	m³/MT NaOH	2 - 2.25
Cooling water	m³/MT NaOH	2.5 - 2.9
Brine purification	kWh/MT NaOH	2.5
Energy required for flaking	kWh/MT NaOH	95 T
Energy required for chlorine liquefaction	kWh/MT NaOH	120 - 200
Energy required @ 6 kA/m² for electrolysis	kWh/MT NaOH	2,060

Benchmarking for Pulp and Paper [3]

Industry Group	Units	Global Avg.	India Avg.	Industry Benchmark
Wood Based Mills	kWh/tonne of paper	1000-1100	1400-1500	1200
	Tonne of steam/tonne of paper	7.0-9.0	12.0-13.0	9
Agro Based Mills	kWh/tonne of paper	1200-1400	1200-1400	1000
	Tonne of steam/tonne of paper	-	12.0-14.0	10
Recycled Fiber Based Mills producing unbleached grades	kWh/tonne of paper	500	450-550	400
	Tonne of steam/tonne of paper	2.5	4.0-5.0	3.5
Recycled Fiber Based Mills producing bleached grades	kWh/tonne of paper	600-650	680-800	570
	Tonne of steam/tonne of paper	4-4.5	6.0-7.0	5

Air conditioned area > 50% built up		Air conditioned area < 50% built up	
Climate zone: Composite			
EPI (kWh/m²/yr.)	Star Label	EPI (kWh/m²/yr.)	Star Label
190-165	1 Star	80-70	1 Star
165 — 140	2 Star	70-60	2 Star
140-115	3 Star	60-50	3 Star
115-90	4 Star	50-40	4 Star
Below 90	5 Star	Below 40	5 Star

Notes:

....

....

....

....

....

....

....

....

....

....

....

....

Transformers

These tables can be used to identify the losses in a transformer based on loading, Energy Savings can be identified based on KVA reduction. Losses mentioned below may vary +/- 10% based on OEM & Voltage level

MV/LV Transformer Losses [4]

Rated Power S_r (kVA)	No-Load Loss P_{fe} (kW)	Load Loss @100% Loading- P_{cu} (kW)
Oil type Distribution Transformer MV-LV		
250	0.61	4.5
315	0.72	5.4
400	0.85	6.5
500	1	7.4
630	1.2	8.9
800	1.45	10.6
1000	1.75	13
1250	2.1	16
1600	2.8	18
2000	3.2	21.5
2500	3.7	24
3150	4	33
4000	4.8	38
Cast Resin Distribution Transformer MV-LV		
250	0.95	3.3
315	1.05	4.2
400	1.2	4.8
500	1.45	5.8
630	1	7
800	1.94	8.2
1000	2.25	9.8
1250	3.3	13
1600	4	14.5
2000	4.6	15.5
2500	5.2	17.5
3150	6	19

Oil type distribution transformer

MVA	No load loss (kW)	Load loss (kW)
5	5.5	33
10	7	50
12.5	9	56
20	14	80
31.5	18	110
50	25	125
80	35	200
100	43	245
160	60	320

Oil type generator transformer at power plant, LV Voltage depends on generation voltage

MVA	No Load Loss	Load Loss	Remarks
200	98	308	
265	97	370	420kV
315	108	455	
265	105	330	765kV
315	135	420	

Notes:

....

....

....

....

....

....

....

MV/LV Transformer Losses for Dry type transformer [5]

Rating kVA	Max. Losses at 50% loading W* (Up to 22 kV class)	Max. Losses at 100% loading W* (Up to 22 kV class)	Max. Losses at 50% loading W* (33 kV class)	Max. Losses at 100% loading W* (33 kV class)
250	1,700	4,320	1,970	4,600
315	2,000	5,040	2,400	5,400
400	2,380	6,040	2,900	6,800
500	2,800	7,250	3,300	7,800
630	3,340	8,820	3,950	9,200
800	3,880	10,240	4,650	11,400
1,000	4,500	12,000	5,300	12,800
1,250	5,190	13,870	6,250	14,500
1,600	6,320	16,800	7,500	18,000
2,000	7,500	20,000	8,880	21,400
2,500	9,250	24,750	10,750	26,500
1,250	5,190	13,870	6,250	14,500
1,600	6,320	16,800	7,500	18,000
2,000	7,500	20,000	8,880	21,400
2,500	9,250	24,750	10,750	26,500

MV/LV ABB Transformer typical inrush currents (kA) for oil transformers [4]

S_{nTR} [kVA]	$K_i = I_{rush}/I_{nTR}$	T_{inrush} [s]
100	14	0.15
160	12	0.2
250	12	0.22
400	12	0.25
630	11	0.3
1000	10	0.35
1600	9	0.4
2000	8	0.45

MV/LV ABB Transformer typical inrush currents (kA) for Cast resin transformer [4]

S_{nTR} [kVA]	$K_i = I_{rush}/I_{nTR}$	T_{inrush} [s]
200	10.5	0.15
250	10.5	0.18
315	10	0.2
400-500	10	0.25
630	10	0.26
800-1000	10	0.3
1250	10	0.35
1600	10	0.4
2000	9.5	0.4

S_{nTR} is the rated power of the transformers.
I_{inrush} is the inrush current of the transformers.
I_{nTR} primary rated current of the transformers.
T_{inrush} time constant of the inrush current.

Notes:

....

....

....

....

....

....

....

....

Motors

These tables can be used to identify energy saving proposals for converting a DC motor to AC motor based on Torque and converting IE2 to higher energy efficiency motors.

As per IEC 60034 the below table is valid for Slip Ring Induction Motor & Squirrel cage Induction motor.

Typical Efficiency of LV Induction Motor [6]

Output	IE2 High Efficiency				IE3 Premium Efficiency				IE4 Super Efficiency			
kw/RPM	3000	1500	1000	750	3000	1500	1000	750	3000	1500	1000	750
15	90.3	90.6	89.7	88	91.9	92.1	91.2	89.6	93.3	93.9	92.9	91.2
18.5	90.9	91.2	90.4	88.6	92.4	92.6	91.7	90.1	93.7	94.2	93.4	91.7
22	91.3	91.6	90.9	89.1	92.7	93	92.2	90.6	94	94.5	93.7	92.1
30	92	92.3	91.7	89.8	93.3	93.6	92.9	91.3	94.5	94.9	94.2	92.7
37	92.5	92.7	92.2	90.3	93.7	93.9	93.3	91.8	94.8	95.2	94.5	93.1
45	92.9	93.1	92.7	90.7	94	94.2	93.7	92.2	95	95.4	94.8	93.4
55	93.2	93.5	93.1	91	94.3	94.6	94.1	92.5	95.3	95.7	95.1	93.7
75	93.8	94	93.7	91.6	94.7	95	94.6	93.1	95.6	96	95.4	94.2
90	94.1	94.2	94	91.9	95	95.2	94.9	93.4	95.8	96.1	95.6	94.4
110	94.3	94.5	94.3	92.3	95.2	95.4	95.1	93.7	96	96.3	95.8	94.7
132	94.6	94.7	94.6	92.6	95.4	95.6	95.4	94	96.2	96.4	96	94.9
160	94.8	94.9	94.8	93	95.6	95.8	95.6	94.3	96.3	96.6	96.2	95.1
200	95	95.1	95	93.5	95.8	96	95.8	94.6	96.5	96.7	96.3	95.4
250	95	95.1	95	93.5	95.8	96	95.8	94.6	96.5	96.7	96.5	95.4
315	95	95.1	95	93.5	95.8	96	95.8	94.6	96.5	96.7	96.6	95.4
355	95	95.1	95	93.5	95.8	96	95.8	94.6	96.5	96.7	96.6	95.4
400	95	95.1	95	93.5	95.8	96	95.8	94.6	96.5	96.7	96.6	95.4
450	95	95.1	95	93.5	95.8	96	95.8	94.6	96.5	96.7	96.6	95.4
500-1000	95	95.1	95	93.5	95.8	96	95.8	94.6	96.5	96.7	96.6	95.4

Output	Speed	100% Load	75% Load	50% Load	Power factor	Torque
kW	RPM	η	η	η	Φ	Nm
0.25	1440	73.5	70.1	63.8	0.64	1.7
0.37	1441	77.3	74.9	69.8	0.66	2.5
0.55	1445	80.8	80.8	78.1	0.75	3.6
0.75	1427	82.5	82.7	81.5	0.78	5
1.1	1434	84.1	83.5	82.1	0.73	7.3
1.5	1439	85.3	84.7	82.7	0.78	10
2.2	1437	86.7	87.6	87	0.83	14.6
3	1440	87.7	88	87.5	0.82	19.9
4	1449	88.6	88.7	87.9	0.8	26.5
5.5	1458	89.6	90.2	90.1	0.81	36
7.5	1456	90.4	90.9	90.6	0.82	49
11	1477	91.4	91.8	91.1	0.82	71.3
15	1472	92.1	92.4	92.1	0.82	97
18.5	1470	92.6	92.8	92.4	0.79	120
22	1470	93	93.2	92.9	0.82	143
30	1481	93.6	94	93.5	0.82	193
37	1479	93.9	94.4	94.3	0.84	239
45	1481	94.2	94.3	94	0.81	290
55	1479	94.6	94.7	94	0.83	352
75	1481	95	95.2	95.1	0.83	484
90	1482	95.2	95.3	95.2	0.85	580
110	1489	95.4	95.4	94.8	0.85	705
132	1488	95.6	95.8	95.3	0.86	847
160	1488	95.8	96	95.8	0.85	1026
200	1487	96	96.4	96.4	0.86	1284
250	1491	96	96	95.6	0.86	1601
315	1491	96	96	95.6	0.86	2018
355	1490	96	96.2	95.8	0.86	2273

Output	Speed	100% Load	75% Load	50% Load	Power factor	Torque
kW	RPM	η	η	η	Φ	Nm
0.55	1449	83.9	84.3	82.6	0.81	3.6
2.2	1465	89.5	90.9	89.5	0.8	14.4
3	1464	90.4	91.1	90.7	0.81	19.8
4	1461	91.1	91.7	91.3	0.79	26.4
5.5	1475	91.9	91.9	91	0.79	35.6
7.5	1473	92.6	92.9	92.1	0.8	48.6
11	1478	93.3	93.6	93	0.77	71.1
15	1476	93.9	94.1	93.8	0.74	97.1
18.5	1484	94.2	94.3	93.5	0.81	119
22	1484	94.5	94.6	94	0.82	142
30	1488	94.9	94.9	94.1	0.75	193
37	1483	95.2	95.5	95.3	0.83	239
45	1481	95.4	95.7	95.6	0.82	290
55	1485	95.7	95.8	95.3	0.85	354
75	1487	96	96.4	96.1	0.86	481
90	1486	96.1	96.3	96.1	0.84	580
110	1491	96.3	96.4	96	0.85	705
132	1489	96.4	96.6	96.1	0.84	846
160	1490	96.6	96.8	96.5	0.86	1026
200	1490	96.7	96.9	96.7	0.86	1282
250	1490	96.7	96.9	96.6	0.85	1601
315	1490	96.7	96.9	96.8	0.83	2018
355	1491	96.7	96.9	96.6	0.85	2271

LV DC Motor Parameters as per IEC 60034-1 [8]

Rated output in kW At 1500 RPM	Rated Armature Current (A)	Field Power in Watts (W)	Efficiency in % (η)	Max Field Weakening Speed. (RPM)	Max Safe Mechanical Speed (RPM)	Rated Torque in Nm (Nm)
15	41	616	80	2400	4600	95.5
20	52.7	968	83	2200	4600	127.3
22.5	59	968	84	2200	4600	143.2
30	78	1694	83	3000	4100	191
40	105	1276	84	2350	4100	254.6
50	131	1276	85	2700	4000	318.3
56	147	1276	85	1950	4100	356.5
60	158	1474	85	3000	4100	381.9
70	176	2310	88	3400	3600	445.6
75	189	2310	88	3400	3600	477.4
80	201	2310	88	3300	3600	509.2
90	228	2376	88	3300	3600	572.9
100	253	2376	88	3300	3600	636.5
115	292	2310	88	2800	3200	732
135	338	2640	89	3100	3200	859.3
150	374	2640	90	3050	3200	954.8
158	394	2640	90	3050	3200	1005.7
180	444	2860	91	2650	3000	1145.8
210	513	3190	92	2320	3000	1336.7
225	552	3190	91	2320	3000	1432.2
235	571	3300	92	2250	2500	1495.9
280	682	3300	92	2025	2500	1782.3
295	719	3300	92	2100	2500	1877.8
325	790	3520	93	2100	2500	2068.7
400	965	4752	93	2050	2300	2546.1
450	1080	5400	94	2000	2300	2864.4
390	960	3400	95	2000	2200	2482.5
550	1295	3700	96	2000	2200	3501
550*	1295	4300	96	2000	2200	4200

LV Adjustable Speed Drive Part load Efficiency (VFD Efficiency).
This table can be used to identify energy saving proposals for sizing VFD & motor based on motor running condition

Variable Drive hp Rating	Efficiency (%)						
	Load, Percentage of Drive Rated Output						
	1.6 %	12.5%	25%	42%	50%	75%	100%
5	35	80	88	91	92	94	95
10	41	83	90	93	94	95	96
20	47	86	93	94	95	96	97
30	50	88	93	95	95	96	97
50	46	86	92	95	95	96	97
60	51	87	92	95	95	96	97
75	47	86	93	95	96	97	97
100	55	89	94	95	96	97	97
200	61	81	95	96	96	97	97

Motor Performance with an unbalanced Utilization Voltage [9]
This table can be used to identify energy saving proposals on improving power quality.

% Voltage Unbalance	Winding Temp °C	I^{2}R Losses (% of Total)	Efficiency Reduction, %	Expected Winding Life, years
0	120	30	--	20
1	130	33	Up to ½%	10
2	140	35	1 to 2%	5
3	150	38	2 to 3%	2.5
4	160	40	3 to 4%	1.25
5	180	45	5% or more	Less than 1

Effect of Applied Voltage Variation on Motor Performance - IEEE 141-1993 Standard [10]

Motor Characteristic	90% of Rated Voltage	110% of Rated Voltage
Starting and Maximum Running Torque	-19%	21%
Starting Current	-10%	10%
Full-Load Current	+5% to +10%	-5% to -10%
Full-Load Efficiency	-1% to -3%	+1% to +3%
Full-Load Power Factor	+3% to +7%	-2% to -7%
Percent Slip	22%	-19%

% Harmonic – Voltage in MV and LV Distribution IEC 61000 [1]

Odd Harmonic Not Multiples of 3			Odd Harmonic Multiples of 3	
Harmonic Order n (Odd Non-Multiples of 3)	Harmonic Voltage % LV/MV (Odd Non-Multiples of 3)	Harmonic Voltage % HV (Odd Non-Multiples of 3)	Harmonic Order n (Odd Multiples of 3)	Harmonic Voltage % LV/MV (Odd Multiples of 3)
5	6	2	3	5
7	5	2	9	1.5
11	3.5	1.5	15	0.3
13	3	1.5	21	0.2
17	2	1	> 21	0.2
19	1.5	1		
23	1.5	0.7		
25	1.5	0.7		
> 25	0.2 + 12.5/n	0.1 + 2.5/n		

Typical Losses in an Induction Motor [11]

Loss Type	Percentage	Formula
Iron losses in core	18%	$P_{iron}=k_h \cdot f \cdot B_{max2} \cdot V$
Windage & friction losses	10%	Depends on System
Stator copper losses	34%	$P_{cu(stator)}=I2 \cdot R_{stator}$
Rotor losses	24%	$P_{cu(rotor)}=I2 \cdot R_{rotor}$
Stray load losses	14%	Depends on Motor

Typical Stray Losses in a Induction Motor [12]

Motor Rating (HP)	Stray Losses - IEEE (%)
1 - 125 HP	0.90%
125.1 - 500 HP	1.20%
501 - 2499 HP	1.50%
2500 and above	1.80%

Allowable Number of Motor Starts and Minimum Time between starts. [9]

For 1800 RPM NEMA Design B Motor		
Motor Rating, hp	Maximum Starts per Hour	Minimum Off-Time Between Starts, seconds
5	16.3	42
10	12.5	46
25	8.8	58
50	6.8	72
100	5.2	110

Analysis of Motor Failures [13]

Reason for Motor Failure	Percentage
Bearing	51%
External	16%
Stator winding	16%
Unknown	10%
Rotor bar	5%
Shaft/coupling	2%

Types of Harmonics and Effects of Harmonics on Motors

Positive Sequence (3n+1)	Negative Sequence (3n+2)	Zero Sequence (3n+3)
Fundamental	2nd Harmonic	3rd Harmonic
4th Harmonic	5th Harmonic	6th Harmonic
7th Harmonic	8th Harmonic	9th Harmonic
10th Harmonic	11th Harmonic	12th Harmonic

- Third Harmonic (and multiples of three): Harmonics that are multiples of three (triplen harmonics like the 3rd, 9th, 15th, etc.) add together in the neutral conductor because they are in-phase in each of the three phases. In systems where the neutral is shared across multiple phases, this can lead to excessive current in the neutral conductor, potentially causing overheating.
- Fifth Harmonic: The fifth harmonic can lead to negative sequence currents, which create a reverse rotating magnetic field in the motor. This reverse field fights against the main rotating field (produced by the fundamental frequency), which can cause increased stress on the motor, overheating, increased losses, and reduced efficiency. The torque produced by the fifth harmonic will try to turn the motor in the opposite direction to normal rotation.

While general purpose alternating-current polyphase, 2-, 4-, 6-, and 8-pole, 60 hertz medium induction motors are not designed to operate at 50 hertz circuits, they are capable of being operated satisfactorily on 50 hertz circuits if their voltage and horsepower ratings are appropriately reduced. When such 60 hertz motors are operated on 50 hertz circuits, the applied voltage at 50 hertz should be reduced to 5/6 of the 60 hertz voltage rating of the motor, and the horsepower load at 50 hertz should be reduced to 5/6 of the 60 hertz horsepower rating of the motor. When a 60 hertz motor is operated on 50 hertz at 5/6 of the 60 hertz voltage and horsepower ratings, the other performance characteristics for 50 hertz operation are as follows:

Speed

The synchronous speed will be 5/6 of the 60 hertz synchronous speed, and the slip will be 5/6 of the 60 hertz slip.

Torques

The rated load torque in pound-feet will be approximately the same as the 60 hertz rated load torque

Service Factor

The service factor will be 1.0.

Should voltages be unbalanced, the rated horsepower of the motor should be multiplied by the factor shown below figure to reduce the possibility of damage to the motor. Operation of the motor above a 5% voltage unbalance condition is not recommended.

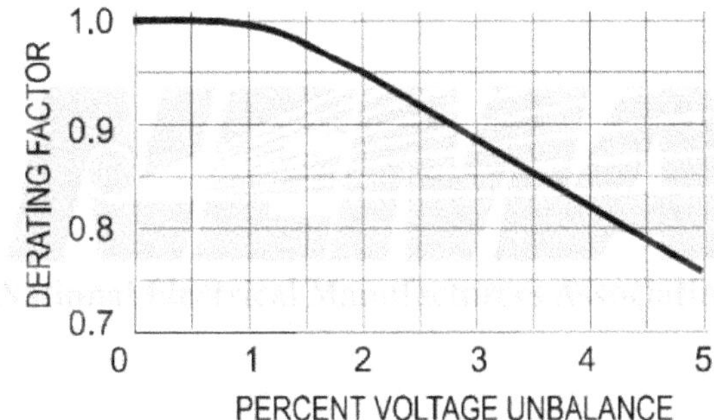

Notes:

Capacitor

Switching technologies for MV capacitor banks [14]

Simulated situation	Additional inductor	Maximum inrush current (peak kA)	Maximum overvoltage (peak p.u.)
No damping added	—	13.6	1.8
Limiting inductor	2.5 mH	2	1.64
Pre-insertion resistor	—	4.5	1.18
Synchronized circuit-breaker	60 µH	3.2	1.26
DS1 diode-based switch	—	1	1.08

ABB Motors , kVAr Compensation at Motor terminals [4]

P.	Q.	Before		After	
(kW)	[kvar]	PF	I [A]	PF	I [A]
400 V/50 Hz/4 poles / 1500 r/min					
7.5	2.5	0.86	14.2	0.96	12.7
11	5	0.81	21.5	0.96	18.2
15	5	0.84	28.5	0.95	25.3
18.5	7.5	0.84	35	0.96	30.5
22	10	0.83	41	0.97	35.1
30	15	0.83	56	0.98	47.5
37	15	0.84	68	0.97	59.1
45	20	0.83	83	0.97	71.1
55	20	0.86	98	0.97	86.9
75	20	0.86	135	0.95	122.8
90	20	0.87	158	0.94	145.9
110	30	0.87	192	0.96	174.8
132	40	0.87	232	0.96	209.6
160	40	0.86	282	0.94	257.4
200	50	0.86	351	0.94	320.2
250	50	0.87	430	0.94	399.4
315	60	0.87	545	0.93	507.9

Rated Power S_r (kVA)	Required kVAr Compensation for transformer at respective Loading (LV Side Compensation only)				
	0	25%	50%	75%	100%
Oil type Distribution Transformer MV-LV					
250	5.2	5.8	7.4	10	14
315	6.3	7	9.1	13	10
400	7.6	8.5	11	16	22
500	9.4	11	14	20	28
630	11	13	17	25	35
800	14	16	25	40	60
1000	16	20	31	49	74
1250	20	24	38	61	93
1600	24	30	47	77	118
2000	24	31	53	90	142
2500	27	37	64	111	175
3150	34	48	89	157	252
4000	56	73	125	212	333
Cast Resin Distribution Transformer MV-LV					
250	4.4	5.3	8.1	13	19
315	5.3	6.4	9.9	16	24
400	5.9	7.3	12	19	29
500	6.8	8.7	14	23	36
630	8	10	17	29	45
800	8.6	12	20	35	56
1000	9.7	13	25	43	69
1250	11	15	29	52	85
1600	14	20	38	67	109
2000	15	23	45	82	134
2500	17	26	54	101	166
3150	18	34	81	159	269

For MV Compensation STATCOM or Synchronous Condenser is preferred.

$$KVAr = k \times kW$$

Current PF/ Desired PF	k					
	0.95	0.96	0.97	0.98	0.99	1
0.50	1.403	1.440	1.481	1.529	1.589	1.732
0.51	1.358	1.395	1.436	1.484	1.544	1.687
0.52	1.314	1.351	1.392	1.440	1.500	1.643
0.53	1.271	1.308	1.349	1.397	1.457	1.600
0.54	1.230	1.267	1.308	1.356	1.416	1.559
0.55	1.190	1.227	1.268	1.316	1.376	1.519
0.60	1.004	1.041	1.082	1.130	1.190	1.333
0.61	0.970	1.007	1.048	1.096	1.156	1.299
0.62	0.937	0.974	1.015	1.063	1.123	1.266
0.63	0.904	0.941	0.982	1.030	1.090	1.233
0.64	0.872	0.909	0.950	0.998	1.068	1.201
0.65	0.840	0.877	0.918	0.966	1.026	1.169
0.70	0.691	0.728	0.769	0.817	0.877	1.020
0.71	0.663	0.700	0.741	0.789	0.849	0.992
0.73	0.607	0.644	0.685	0.733	0.793	0.936
0.74	0.580	0.617	0.658	0.706	0.766	0.909
0.75	0.553	0.590	0.631	0.679	0.739	0.882
0.81	0.395	0.432	0.473	0.521	0.581	0.724
0.82	0.369	0.406	0.447	0.495	0.555	0.698
0.83	0.343	0.380	0.421	0.469	0.529	0.672
0.84	0.317	0.354	0.395	0.443	0.503	0.646
0.85	0.291	0.328	0.369	0.417	0.477	0.620
0.90	0.155	0.192	0.233	0.281	0.341	0.484
0.91	0.127	0.164	0.205	0.253	0.313	0.456
0.92	0.097	0.134	0.175	0.223	0.283	0.426
0.93	0.066	0.103	0.144	0.192	0.252	0.395
0.94	0.034	0.071	0.112	0.160	0.220	0.363
0.95	0.000	0.037	0.079	0.126	0.186	0.329

Industrial Cables

Current Ratings of PVC Insulated Aluminium Conductor [15]

Nominal Size of Cable (Sq. mm)	3, 3.5 & 4 Core PVC Insulated & Sheathed Cables as per IS - 1554 (Part-1)		
	In Ground (Amp)	In Air (Amp)	Approx Voltage Drop (mv / amp / mtr)
16	61	52	3.96
25	78	70	2.49
35	94	85	1.8
50	111	104	1.34
70	136	131	0.93
95	163	162	0.68
120	185	186	0.54
150	206	212	0.45
185	234	245	0.36
240	271	291	0.29
300	305	335	0.25
400	348	390	0.21

Current Ratings of XLPE Insulated Conductor [15]

Nominal Size of Cable (Sq. mm)	3, 3.5 & 4 Core XLPE Insulated & Sheathed Cables as per IS - 7098 (Part-1)		
	In Ground (Amp)	In Air (Amp)	Approx Voltage Drop (Mv / amp / mtr)
16	74	69	4.24
25	95	93	2.67
35	114	114	1.94
50	134	138	1.43
70	164	175	0.99
95	197	216	0.72
120	223	249	0.58
150	249	284	0.48
185	282	329	0.39
240	327	392	0.31
300	369	452	0.26
400	420	526	0.21

Current rating (D.C.) for Two single core cable with XLPE Insulation and rated voltage 1500 V [15]

Size (Sq.mm)	Buried Direct in the Ground (A)		In Single-Way Ducts (A)		In Air (A)	
	Copper	Aluminium	Copper	Aluminium	Copper	Aluminium
16	115	89	97	75	108	84
25	148	115	124	96	144	112
35	177	137	148	115	176	137
50	208	161	174	135	212	165
70	255	198	213	165	269	209
95	314	243	258	200	342	265
120	358	278	293	227	399	310
150	401	310	328	254	455	352
185	455	352	371	288	528	409
240	528	409	431	334	628	487
300	598	463	487	377	726	561
400	687	533	558	433	857	664
500	790	613	640	497	1008	782
630	911	705	736	570	1189	921
800	1046	809	843	652	1398	1082
1000	1190	923	956	741	1629	1264

Derating factor for variation in ambient air for cables [15]

Air/Ground Temperature (°C)	Derating Factor		
	Free Air	Direct Buried	Ducts
15	1.14	1.12	1.12
30	1.1	1.08	1.08
35	1.05	1.04	1.04
40	1	1	1
45	0.96	0.96	0.96
50	0.89	0.91	0.91
55	0.87	0.87	0.87

Nominal Size of Conductor (Sq. mm)	Max D.C. Resistance at 20°C (Ohm/Km)		A.C. Resistance at 90°C (Ohm/Km)	
	Copper	Aluminium	Copper	Aluminium
16	1.15	1.91	1.47	2.44
25	0.727	1.2	0.93	1.54
35	0.524	0.868	0.668	1.11
50	0.387	0.641	0.494	0.82
70	0.268	0.443	0.342	0.568
95	0.193	0.32	0.247	0.41
120	0.153	0.253	0.196	0.325
150	0.124	0.206	0.159	0.264
185	0.0991	0.164	0.128	0.211
240	0.0754	0.125	0.0985	0.161
300	0.0601	0.1	0.0796	0.129
400	0.0477	0.0778	0.0637	0.101
500	0.0366	0.0605	0.0515	0.0786
630	0.0283	0.0469	0.0421	0.0615
800	0.0221	0.0367	0.0354	0.0488
1000	0.0176	0.0291	0.0225	0.0372

Derating Factor for two single core cable laid in ground, horizontal formation (DC) [15]

# of circuits	Touching	150mm	300mm	450mm	600mm
2	0.8	0.85	0.9	0.92	0.95
3	0.7	0.78	0.85	0.88	0.91
4	0.64	0.73	0.81	0.86	0.89
5	0.59	0.7	0.79	0.84	0.88
6	0.55	0.67	0.77	0.83	0.87
7	0.53	0.65	0.76	0.82	0.86
8	0.51	0.64	0.75	0.82	0.86
9	0.49	0.63	0.74	0.81	0.85
10	0.48	0.63	0.74	0.81	0.85
11	0.47	0.62	0.73	0.8	0.84
12	0.46	0.61	0.73	0.8	0.84

Derating Factor for multi core cable laid in ground, horizontal formation [15]

# of circuits	Touching	150mm	300mm	450mm	600mm
2	0.8	0.84	0.87	0.9	0.91
3	0.68	0.74	0.79	0.83	0.86
4	0.62	0.69	0.75	0.8	0.83
5	0.58	0.65	0.72	0.77	0.8
6	0.55	0.62	0.69	0.75	0.78
7	0.52	0.59	0.67	0.73	0.77
8	0.5	0.57	0.66	0.72	0.75
9	0.48	0.55	0.65	0.71	0.75
10	0.46	0.54	0.64	0.7	0.74
11	0.45	0.53	0.63	0.7	0.74
12	0.44	0.52	0.62	0.69	0.73

Derating Factor for three core cable laid in duct, horizontal formation [15]

Number of Cables	Touching	150mm	300mm	450mm	600mm
2	0.85	0.87	0.9	0.92	0.94
3	0.75	0.79	0.83	0.86	0.88
4	0.69	0.74	0.79	0.83	0.86
5	0.65	0.7	0.76	0.8	0.84
6	0.62	0.67	0.73	0.79	0.83
7	0.59	0.65	0.72	0.78	0.82
8	0.57	0.63	0.7	0.77	0.81
9	0.55	0.62	0.69	0.76	0.8
10	0.54	0.61	0.68	0.75	-
11	0.52	0.6	0.68	0.75	-
12	0.51	0.59	0.67	0.74	-

A.W.G.	Diameter (mm)	Cross-Sectional Area (mm²)
0000	11.68	107.3
000	10.4	85
00	9.27	67.4
0	8.25	53.5
2	6.54	33.6
4	5.19	21.2
6	4.12	13.3
8	3.25	8.4
10	2.59	5.3
12	2.05	3.3
14	1.63	2.1
16	1.29	1.3
18	1.02	0.8
20	0.81	0.5
22	0.64	0.3
24	0.51	0.2

Note: The American Wire Gauge (AWG) was originally known as the Brown & Sharp (B&S) Gauge and both terms are synonymous. The gauge number can apply to a single wire or to a stranded or bunched conductor. The cross-sectional areas given apply to single wire only. The larger gauges are sometimes written using a number to denote the number of zeroes, e.g. 0 gauge can be written 1/0 and 000 as 3/0.

Notes:

....

....

....

....

....

....

Motor Full-Load Current ≤ (AC)	Motor Full-Load Current ≤ (DC)	Minimum Size of Grounding Conductor Termination Attachment Means, AWG	Minimum Size of Screw, Stud, or Bolt (Steel)	Minimum Size of Screw, Stud, or Bolt (Bronze)
12	12	14	#6	—
16	16	12	#8	—
30	40	10	#10	—
45	68	8	#12	#10
70	105	6	5/16"	#12
110	165	4	5/16"	5/16"
160	240	3	3/8"	5/16"
250	375	1	1/2"	3/8"
400	600	2/0	—	1/2"
600	900	3/0	—	1/2"

Notes:

....

....

....

....

....

....

....

....

....

....

Typical power factors of some electrical equipment [4]

Load	$\cos\varphi$ power factor
Transformers (no load condition)	0.1-0.15
Motor	0.7-0.85
Metal working apparatuses: Arc welding	0.35-0.6
Metal working apparatuses: Arc welding compensated	0.7-0.8
Metal working apparatuses: Resistance welding	0.4-0.6
Metal working apparatuses: Arc melting furnace	0.75-0.9
Fluorescent lamps: compensated	0.9
Fluorescent lamps: uncompensated	0.4-0.6
AC DC converters	0.6-0.95
DC drives	0.4-0.75
AC drives	0.95-0.97
Resistive load	1

UPS

UPS Efficiency at different loads.
The following table was extracted from Schneider Electric Online Tool

Load	10-1000kVA			
	Double Conversion	Delta Conversion	Modular UPS (Delta Conversion)	Eco Mode
25%	95.4	88 - 91.5	95.3	99
50%	95.5	93 - 95	96.3	99.3
75%	95.1	95 - 96	96.4	99.3
100%	94.6	96.1- 96.4	96.2	99.3

Notes:

....

....

....

....

....

Gearless Conveyor Drives (GCDs) in Industrial Applications

Gearless Conveyor Drives (GCDs) offer a modern solution in conveyor drive technology with enhanced efficiency, reliability, and reduced maintenance. Developed by leading companies like ABB and Siemens, these systems employ low-speed synchronous motors that directly drive conveyor belts, eliminating the need for high-speed motors, gearboxes, and couplings. This streamlined mechanical design reduces the number of mechanical wear components, which in turn decreases maintenance demands and increases system availability.

The lack of gearboxes not only simplifies the mechanical structure but also increases energy efficiency. These drives are particularly effective in applications requiring high throughput and adaptability to varying elevations along the conveyor path. The direct connection of the motor to the conveyor shaft ensures optimal power transmission, leading to significant energy savings and a reduction in operational costs.

GCDs are equipped with sophisticated monitoring and diagnostics capabilities that facilitate early detection of potential issues, allowing for proactive maintenance. This capability, coupled with a simpler mechanical setup, leads to a reduction in downtime and operational disruptions. Furthermore, the compact design of gearless systems allows for more flexible installation options, particularly beneficial in constrained spaces like tunnels or underground settings.

Application: Mining, bulk material handling, and port facilities.

Industry: Mining, material handling, infrastructure.

Electric Linear Actuators

Replacing hydraulic actuators with electric linear actuators offers various benefits, particularly in terms of energy efficiency and control. Electric actuators utilize electrical power to create motion, eliminating the need for hydraulic fluids and reducing potential environmental hazards associated with leaks and disposals. They also provide precise control over speed, position, and torque, enhancing operational accuracy.

Electric linear actuators can integrate seamlessly with modern control systems, enabling automation and real-time adjustments based on sensor inputs. This adaptability is crucial in dynamic environments where conditions change rapidly. Additionally, electric actuators are generally quieter and require less maintenance than hydraulic systems, reducing downtime and overall operating costs.

Application: Hydraulic Lifts, Doors.

Industry: Iron and Steel and Various Industries.

Step 1: Finding Force, Travel distance, Travel Time, Retraction Time

Force applied on Load by Hydraulic $(\text{F}) = (A_1 \times P_1) - (A_2 \times P_2)$

1. Force (F) is in lbf
2. Area (A) in sq.in
3. Pressure (P) in PSI

Step 2: Choosing the right Linear Actuator

Comparision between Electric Linear Actuators and Hydraulic

Regenerative Braking

There are two main types of regenerative systems - active front end (AFE) and regenerative braking units. AFE systems can feed energy back into the grid, while regenerative braking units typically redirect energy to other loads within the same system. The choice depends on the specific needs of the application and the potential for energy savings.

Application: Cranes.

Industry: Sugar, Iron and Steel and Various Industries.

Variable Refrigerant Flow (VRF) and Heat Transfer Solution (HTS) Panels

Variable Refrigerant Flow (VRF) systems, also known as Variable Refrigerant Volume (VRV) systems, are sophisticated air conditioning technologies that optimize energy use and provide customized control over indoor climates. These systems utilize refrigerant as both the cooling and heating medium, circulated from a single or multiple outdoor condensing units to various indoor units. By dynamically adjusting the refrigerant flow based on specific area requirements, VRF systems achieve superior energy efficiency and comfort.

Integrating VRF systems with Hybrid Thermal Solar (HTS) panels can significantly enhance energy conservation. HTS panels are innovative solar energy solutions that combine photovoltaic (PV) cells, which convert sunlight into electricity, with thermal technology, which harnesses solar energy for heating. This dual capability not only provides a renewable source of power but also reduces the load on the VRF system by using solar heat for temperature regulation.

Such integration is particularly effective in reducing energy consumption in environments where consistent and efficient temperature control is crucial. HTS panels support sustainable energy use by lessening dependency on conventional power sources and exploiting solar energy, which is abundant and free.

Application: Commercial Buildings, Residential Complexes, Sustainable Developments.

Industry: Renewable Energy, HVAC, Property Development.

Advances in Sustainable Convertor/Inverter Technology

Three phase Static Stabilizers

Static Stabilizers, also known as Static Voltage Stabilizers (SVS), utilize solid-state devices to maintain load voltage stability. Unlike traditional servo stabilizers that mechanically adjust the transformer taps to stabilize the voltage, static stabilizers adjust voltage levels through electronic circuits without any moving parts. This ensures faster response to voltage fluctuations, higher reliability, and reduced maintenance costs. They are widely used in sensitive electronic equipment, medical devices, and industrial applications where precise voltage regulation is crucial.

Application: Various.

Industry: Various Industries.

Direct Torque Control Drives

Direct Torque Control (DTC) Drives are advanced AC drive control techniques used primarily in variable frequency drives to control the torque (and thus the speed) of three-phase AC electric motors. This method provides an almost instant torque control in electric motors, offering a very dynamic response. DTC drives do not require encoders or feedback devices for typical applications, as they can directly estimate the motor's torque and flux conditions. This results in a robust, high-performance drive system with simpler hardware and lower costs.

Application: Various.

Industry: Various Industries.

Electrostatic Motors

1. **Overview and Construction:** Electrostatic motors, also known as capacitor motors, operate on the principle of electrostatic force. These motors utilize a high-voltage electric field to create attraction and repulsion forces that result in movement. The construction of electrostatic motors is markedly different from traditional electromagnetic motors. They consist of electrodes (stators) and a rotor, where the electrodes are arranged around the rotor to generate electrostatic fields when voltage is applied. The rotors can be made of lightweight materials, and because the force is generated through electric fields, these motors can be designed to be very compact and lightweight.

2. **Environmental Impacts:** Electrostatic motors have a relatively low environmental impact due to several factors. Firstly, their construction requires fewer and less hazardous materials compared to conventional motors that might use heavy metals or rare-earth elements. This reduces the environmental degradation associated with material extraction and processing. Secondly, their operational efficiency, while generally lower than electromagnetic motors, can be optimized for specific applications where their unique characteristics (such as high precision and low torque applications) offer advantages. Lastly, the minimal use of hazardous materials and the potential for using sustainable materials in their construction enhance their recyclability and reduce environmental footprint.

Application: Conveyor Belts and Various Applications
Industry: Various Industries.

Synchronous Reluctance Motors (SyRM)

1. **Overview and Construction:** Synchronous Reluctance Motors (SyRMs) are a type of AC motor that operates on the principle of reluctance torque. The rotor in a SyRM is designed to have paths of different magnetic reluctance. When the rotating magnetic field produced by the stator interacts with these paths, torque is generated due to the tendency of the system to minimize reluctance. The construction of SyRMs eliminates the need for permanent magnets, relying instead on a precisely designed rotor structure to generate motion. This results in a motor that is both efficient and robust, capable of operating effectively across a wide range of speeds and loads.

2. **Environmental Impacts:** The environmental impacts of SyRMs are significantly lower than those of conventional motors, especially those that rely on rare-earth magnets. The absence of these magnets in SyRMs means that there is no need for mining rare-earth elements, which is a process associated with significant environmental degradation and pollution. Furthermore, the high efficiency of SyRMs leads to lower energy consumption and operational emissions over the motor's lifetime. The materials used in SyRMs, such as steel and copper, are both abundant and highly recyclable, further reducing the environmental footprint. Additionally, the long operational life and durability of SyRMs contribute to less frequent replacements and reduced waste.

Application: Various Utility Applications
Industry: Various Industries.

Aloe vera Batteries:

Aloe E-cell Aloe Vera Battery operates using an innovative combination of Aloe Vera gel and advanced materials, which work together to create an efficient and eco-friendly primary (non-rechargeable) energy storage solution. To better understand the technology behind Aloe Vera Batteries, we can break down the battery's components and their functions:

1. **Aloe Vera Gel Electrolyte:** Aloe Vera gel serves as a natural electrolyte in the battery. The gel is rich in mucilage, phloem, and other organic compounds that facilitate ionic conductivity. The gel also exhibits high water content and a unique polysaccharide structure, which enable the efficient transfer of ions between the cathode and anode.

2. **Organic Polymer Cathode:** The battery uses organic polymer materials for its cathode. These materials offer improved energy density, better electrochemical stability, and controlled discharge performance compared to traditional inorganic materials used in batteries. The use of organic polymers also contributes to the battery's eco-friendliness and recyclability.

3. **Innovative Separator:** A crucial component of the Aloe Vera Battery is the separator, which keeps the cathode and anode physically separated while allowing ions to flow through the electrolyte. The separator is designed to be thin and porous, maximizing ionic conductivity and minimizing internal resistance. This innovative separator contributes to the battery's overall efficiency and performance.

4. **Unique Internal Design:** The Aloe Vera Battery features a carefully engineered internal design that optimizes the distribution of the Aloe Vera gel electrolyte, the placement of the separator, and the arrangement of the cathode and anode materials. This design ensures consistent performance, uniform current density, and efficient energy storage and release.

5. **Electrochemical Reactions:** In an Aloe Vera Battery, electrochemical reactions occur at the interface between the Aloe Vera gel electrolyte and the cathode/anode materials. During discharge, oxidation takes place at the anode, causing it to release electrons that travel through the external circuit to the cathode. Simultaneously, the Aloe Vera gel electrolyte facilitates the movement of ions between the anode and cathode. At the cathode, a reduction reaction occurs, allowing it to accept the incoming electrons. This continuous flow of electrons and ions generates electrical energy.

Application: low-drain devices.

Industry: Various Industries.

AC Battery

AC Biode Ltd. is developing the first-ever standalone battery based on AC. Biode features the characteristics of both anodes and cathodes. Thanks to a special electric circuit also found in particle accelerators, the system offers more V/Ah flexibility, requires 30% less space, and is safer than every type of regular direct-current (DC) battery. Conventional batteries use DC, which leads to power loss when electricity is converted from AC to DC.

Benefits:
1. Battery is up to 30% more compact and reduces conversion losses
2. Uses existing materials/battery production lines
3. Safer than conventional Li-ion batteries
4. Lower electrical resistance (safer/longer-lasting)

Application: Energy Storage

Industry: Various Industries.

Solid Fuel Type	CO_2 EF
kg CO_2 per short ton	
Coal and Coke	
Anthracite	2,602
Bituminous	2,325
Sub-bituminous	1,676
Lignite	1,389
Mixed (Commercial Sector)	2,016
Mixed (Electric Power Sector)	1,885
Mixed (Industrial Coking)	2,468
Mixed (Industrial Sector)	2,116
Coal Coke	2,819
Other Fuels - Solid	
Municipal Solid Waste	902
Petroleum Coke (Solid)	3,072
Plastics	2,850
Tires	2,407
Biomass Fuels - Solid	
Agricultural Byproducts	975
Peat	895
Solid Byproducts	1,096
Wood and Wood Residuals	1,640
kg CO_2 per scf	
Natural Gas	
Natural Gas	0.05444
Other Fuels - Gaseous	
Blast Furnace Gas	0.02524
Coke Oven Gas	0.02806

Fuel Gas	0.08189
Propane Gas	0.15463
Biomass Fuels - Gaseous	
Landfill Gas	0.025254
Other Biomass Gases	0.034106
kg CO$_2$ per gallon	
Petroleum Products	
Asphalt and Road Oil	11.91
Aviation Gasoline	8.31
Butane	6.67
Butylene	7.22
Crude Oil	10.29
Distillate Fuel Oil No. 1	10.18
Distillate Fuel Oil No. 2	10.21
Distillate Fuel Oil No. 4	10.96
Ethane	4.05
Ethylene	3.83
Heavy Gas Oils	11.09
Isobutane	6.43
Isobutylene	7.09
Kerosene	10.15
Kerosene-Type Jet Fuel	9.75
Liquefied Petroleum Gases (LPG)	5.68
Lubricants	10.69
Motor Gasoline	8.78
Naphtha (<401 deg F)	8.50
Natural Gasoline	7.36
Other Oil (>401 deg F)	10.59
Pentanes Plus	7.70
Petrochemical Feedstocks	8.88

Propane	5.72
Propylene	6.17
Residual Fuel Oil No. 5	10.21
Residual Fuel Oil No. 6	11.27
Special Naphtha	9.04
Unfinished Oils	10.36
Used Oil	10.21
Biomass Fuels - Liquid	
Biodiesel (100%)	9.45
Ethanol (100%)	5.75
Rendered Animal Fat	8.88
Vegetable Oil	9.79

Emission Factors for Greenhouse Gas Inventories- Mobile Combustion [17]

Fuel Type	kg CO_2 Unit	Unit
Aviation Gasoline	8.31	gallon
Biodiesel (100%)	9.45	gallon
Compressed Natural Gas (CNG)	0.05444	scf
Diesel Fuel	10.21	gallon
Ethanol (100%)	5.75	gallon
Kerosene-Type Jet Fuel	9.75	gallon
Liquefied Natural Gas (LNG)	4.50	gallon
Liquefied Petroleum Gases (LPG)	5.68	gallon
Motor Gasoline	8.78	gallon
Residual Fuel Oil	11.27	gallon

Types of Hydrogen

Type of hydrogen	Energy source	Hydrogen production process
Gray hydrogen	Fossil fuels, etc.	CH4, etc. → steam reforming → H2 + CO2 → atmospheric release
Blue hydrogen	Fossil fuels, etc.	CH4, etc. → steam reforming → H2 + CO2 → capture/storage
Turquoise hydrogen	Combustion and waste heat, Electricity	CH4 → direct decomposition → H2 + C → storage and effective utilization, etc.
Green hydrogen	Electricity (renewable energy)	H2O → electrolysis → H2
Purple hydrogen	Heat (nuclear power), Electricity	CH4, etc. → direct decomposition → H2 + C → effective utilization; H2O → High-temperature water electrolysis, etc. → H2

GOI Green Hydrogen Phased Approach

The mission is proposed to be implemented in a phased manner, focusing initially on deployment of Green Hydrogen in sectors that are already using hydrogen, and evolving an ecosystem for R&D, Regulations and Pilot projects.

Phase I (2022-23 TO 2025-26)

The focus of Phase I will be on creating demand while enabling adequate supply by increasing the domestic electrolyser manufacturing capacity. The scale up of Green Hydrogen production and use, and the proposed measures under the Mission in the first phase, are expected to drive down costs, allowing for greater and wider Green Hydrogen deployment in the next phase.

Phase II (2026-27 TO 2029-30)

Green Hydrogen costs are expected to become competitive with fossil-fuel based alternatives in refinery and fertilizer sector by the beginning of the second phase, allowing for accelerated growth in production. Depending upon the evolution of costs and market demand, the potential for taking up commercial scale Green Hydrogen based projects in steel, mobility and shipping sectors will be explored. At the same time, it is proposed to undertake pilot projects in other potential sectors like railways, aviation etc. R&D activities will be scaled up for continuous development of products.

Hydrogen Fueled Powered Power Plants [12]

Researchers at IIT Delhi developed a 'Hydrogen fuelled Spark Ignition Engine Generator for Electricity Generation'. To break it down, the generator uses hydrogen as fuel in the internal combustion engine as opposed to environment-unfriendly diesel. The researchers at Engines and Unconventional fuels Laboratory, IIT Delhi collaborated with Kirloskar Oil Engines Limited (KOEL) and the Research and Development centre of Indian Oil to increase thermal efficiency along with zero emissions. The project was mainly funded by the Ministry of New and Renewable Energy (MNRE), Government of India, and supplementary funding was provided by KOEL and the IOCL R&D Centre.

City	Climate Type	City	Climate Type
Ahmedabad	Hot & Dry	Kurnool	Warm & Humid
Allahabad	Composite	Leh	Cold
Amritsar	Composite	Lucknow	Composite
Aurangabad	Hot & Dry	Ludhiana	Composite
Bangalore	Temperate	Chennai	Warm & Humid
Barmer	Hot & Dry	Manali	Cold
Belgaum	Warm & Humid	Mangalore	Warm & Humid
Bhagalpur	Warm & Humid	Mumbai	Warm & Humid
Bhopal	Composite	Nagpur	Composite
Bhubaneshwar	Warm & Humid	Nellore	Warm & Humid
Bikaner	Hot & Dry	New Delhi	Composite
Chandigarh	Composite	Panjim	Warm & Humid
Chitradurga	Warm & Humid	Patna	Composite
Dehradun	Composite	Pune	Warm & Humid
Dibrugarh	Warm & Humid	Raipur	Composite
Guwahati	Warm & Humid	Rajkot	Composite
Gorakhpur	Composite	Ramgundam	Warm & Humid
Gwalior	Composite	Ranchi	Composite
Hissar	Composite	Ratnagiri	Warm & Humid
Hyderabad	Composite	Raxaul	Warm & Humid
Imphal	Warm & Humid	Saharanpur	Composite
Indore	Composite	Shillong	Cold
Jabalpur	Composite	Sholapur	Hot & Dry
Jagdalpur	Warm & Humid	Srinagar	Cold
Jaipur	Composite	Sundernagar	Cold
Jaisalmer	Hot & Dry	Surat	Hot & Dry
Jalandhar	Composite	Tezpur	Warm & Humid
Jamnagar	Warm & Humid	Tiruchirappalli	Warm & Humid
Jodhpur	Hot & Dry	Trivandrum	Warm & Humid
Jorhat	Warm & Humid	Tuticorin	Warm & Humid
Kochi	Warm & Humid	Udhagamandalam	Cold
Kolkata	Warm & Humid	Vadodara	Hot & Dry
Kota	Hot & Dry	Veraval	Warm & Humid
Kullu	Cold	Vishakhapatnam	Warm & Humid

USEFUL SOFTWARE'S AND CALCULATORS

	Calculator: UPS Comparison **Vendor:** Schneider Electric **Application:** Comparing UPS Efficiency and Savings
	Software: Measur **Vendor:** US Department of Energy **Application:** Motor, Pump and Fan Efficiency
	Calculator: Solar Calculator **Vendor:** Adani **Application:** Estimating Solar kW and Price
	Calculator: Heat Transfer **Vendor:** Watlow **Application:** Air and Water heating
	Calculator: EnergySave **Vendor:** ABB **Application:** VFD for Fan, Pump and Compressed Air

	Calculator: Coolselector2 **Vendor:** Danfoss **Application:** All Industrial requirements
	Calculator: Cable loss Calculator **Vendor:** Energoprom **Application:** For Calculating Cable losses

References

[1] Schneider Electric, "Cahier technique no. 152," Schneider Electric, 1999.

[2] "NEMA Standard : ANSI/NEMA MG 1-2021," National Electrical Manufacturers Association, 2022.

[3] BEE, "Enhancing Energy Efficiency through Industrial Partnership (Outcome and Way forward)," BEE, 2018.

[4] ABB, "Technical Application Papers No.8 - Power factor correction and harmonic," ABB, 2018.

[5] BEE, "ENERGY CONSERVATION BUILDING CODE 2017," BEE, 2020.

[6] ABB, "Low voltage motor guide," 2018, ABB.

[7] ABB, "Low voltage - General performance cast iron motors," ABB, 2024.

[8] Crompton Greaves Limited, "DC Motors," Crompton Greaves Limited, 2011.

[9] US Department of Energy, "PREMIUM EFFICIENCY MOTOR SELECTION AND APPLICATION GUIDE," US Department of Energy, 2014.

[10] US Department of Energy, "Motor Systems Tip Sheet #9," US Department of Energy, USA, 2012.

[11] ABB, "Motor efficiency," ABB.

[12] BEE, Energy Efficiency in Electrical Utilities, Delhi: BEE, 2015.

[13] Electrical Apparatus Service Association, "Effect of Repair/Rewinding on Motor Efficiency," Electrical Apparatus Service Association, London, 2003.

[14] ABB, "Technical Application Papers No. 23 - MEDIUM VOLTAGE CAPACITOR SWITCHING," ABB, 2018.

[15] POLYCAB, "XLPE INSULATED HEAVY DUTY CABLES 650/110V," POLYCAB, 2018.

[16] Tolomatic, "Tolomatic," Tolomatic, 2024. [Online]. Available: https://www.tolomatic.com/wp-content/uploads/2022/05/869-electric-vs-hydraulic-actuators-infographic_update.pdf.

[17] U.S. Environmental Protection Agency, "Emission Factors for Greenhouse Gas Inventories," U.S. Environmental Protection Agency, 2024.

[18] ABB, "Technical Application Papers No. 26 -Medium voltage switching devices:," ABB, 2018.

Notes:

Notes:

Notes:

Notes:

Notes:

Notes: